What Is
Mount Rushmore?

By Laine Falk

Children's Press®
An Imprint of Scholastic Inc.
New York Toronto London Auckland Sydney
Mexico City New Delhi Hong Kong
Danbury, Connecticut

These content vocabulary word builders are for grades 1–2.

Subject Consultant: Eli J. Lesser, MA, Director of Education, National Constitution Center, Philadelphia, Pennsylvania

Reading Consultant: Cecilia Minden-Cupp, PhD, Early Literacy Consultant and Author, Chapel Hill, North Carolina

Photographs © 2009: Alamy Images: 13 bottom right (JupiterImages), 13 bottom left (Craig Lovell/Eagle Visions Photography), back cover, 15 bottom (Buddy Mays), 17 (L. Zacharie); Animals Animals: 23 bottom right (Erwin & Peggy Bauer), 23 top right (Mark Chappell); AP Images: 20 bottom (Charles Bennett), 15 top (Charlie Riedel), 9 top, 11 bottom right, 11 top left; Corbis Images: 4 bottom right, 16 (Dave Bartruff), 23 bottom left (George D. Lepp), 1, 19 (Joseph Sohm/Visions of America), 4 top, 5 top left, 5 bottom left, 5 top right, 8, 9 bottom left, 10, 11 bottom left (Underwood & Underwood); Digital Railroad/Craig Lovell/Stock Connection: 13 top right, 13 bottom left; Getty Images/Alfred Eisenstaedt/Pix Inc.: 11 top right; Landov, LLC/Friedel Gierth/dpa: 2, 5 bottom right, 12, 20 top; Minden Pictures/Michael Quinton: 23 top left; Courtesy of National Park Service/Rise Studio, Rapid City, SD: 9 bottom right; Photoshot/Mauritius World Pictures: 7 main; Superstock, Inc./Prisma: 4 bottom left, 6; VEER/Alloy Photography: cover. Maps by James McMahon

Series Design: Simonsays Design!
Art Direction, Production, and Digital Imaging: Scholastic Classroom Magazines

Library of Congress Cataloging-in-Publication Data

Falk, Laine, 1974-
What Is Mount Rushmore? / Laine Falk.
    p. cm. – (Scholastic news nonfiction readers)
Includes bibliographical references and index.
ISBN 13: 978-0-531-21090-1 (lib. bdg.)   978-0-531-22427-4 (pbk.)
ISBN 10: 0-531-21090-1 (lib. bdg.)   0-531-22427-9 (pbk.)
1. Mount Rushmore National Memorial (S.D.)–Juvenile literature. I. Title. II. Series.
F657.R8F35 2009
978.3'93–dc22   2008027082

CONTENTS

WORD HUNT

Look for these words as you read. They will be in **bold**.

carve
(karv)

mountain
(**moun**-tuhn)

rangers
(**rayn**-jurz)

granite
(**gran**-it)

model
(**mod**-uhl)

sculptor
(**skuhlp**-tur)

sculpture
(**skuhlp**-chur)

5

What Is Mount Rushmore?

Mount Rushmore is a **mountain**. It has the faces of four Presidents on it. They are Washington, Jefferson, Roosevelt, and Lincoln.

mountain

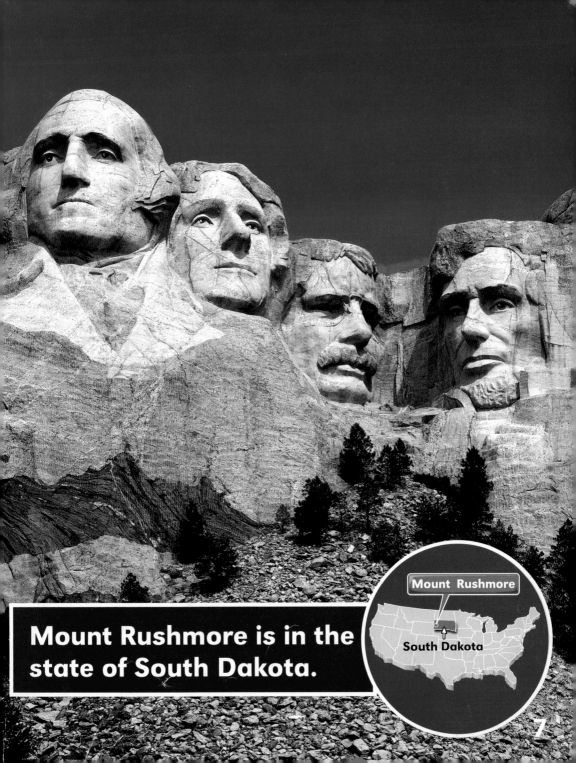

Mount Rushmore is in the state of South Dakota.

Mount Rushmore

South Dakota

A **sculptor** made the faces. His name was Gutzon Borglum (GOOT-zuhn BOR-glum). He made a small **model** before he worked on the mountain.

sculptor

model

**The sculptor practiced on models.
Then he was ready for the mountain!**

The mountain is made of hard stone called **granite**. About 400 workers helped **carve**, or cut, the faces.

carve

granite

Workers used ropes and pulleys to move up and down the mountain.

The work was hard and slow. It took 14 years. At last the giant faces were finished!

This great **sculpture** helps people remember four of our great Presidents.

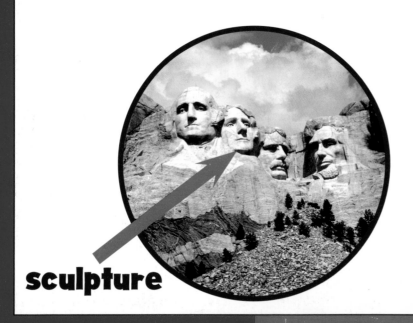

sculpture

George Washington

Thomas Jefferson

Theodore Roosevelt

Abraham Lincoln

13

Over the years, the faces on the mountain got dirty.

In 2005, workers gave them a bath. They used hoses to wash the sculpture. It took them about three weeks to get the faces clean.

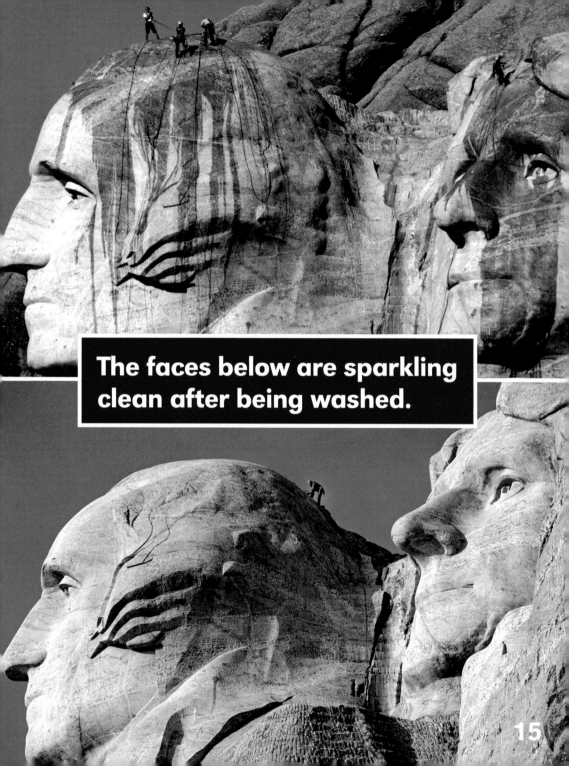

The faces below are sparkling clean after being washed.

15

Visitors come from all over the world to see Mount Rushmore.

Rangers help care for the mountain. They tell people the story of the sculpture.

rangers

GRAND VIEW TERRACE

The Fourth of July is our nation's birthday. It is a special day at Mount Rushmore. Fireworks light up the sky above the four Presidents. The fireworks celebrate America, just like this great sculpture!

MOUNT RUSHMORE

Visitors to Mount Rushmore can see another giant sculpture nearby. It is of Crazy Horse, an Indian Chief.

The Sculpture	How big is the sculpture?
Mount Rushmore 	The faces are 60 feet tall. That's about as tall as 3 giraffes.
Crazy Horse 	The sculpture will be 563 feet tall. That's about as tall as 28 giraffes.

AND CRAZY HORSE

That one will be the largest sculpture in the world when it is finished! The chart below compares the two sculptures.

What does the sculpture show?	How long did it take to create?
The sculpture shows the faces of four U.S. Presidents.	The sculpture took 14 years to complete, from 1927 to 1941.
The sculpture will show Crazy Horse from the waist up, and the head of his horse.	The sculpture was begun more than 60 years ago. It is still not complete.

YOUR NEW WORDS

carve (karv) to cut a shape out of a piece of wood, stone, or other material

granite (**gran**-it) a hard rock used for buildings or art

model (**mod**-uhl) a small copy of a bigger object

mountain (**moun**-tuhn) a very high piece of land

rangers (**rayn**-jurz) people who take care of a park or a forest

sculptor (**skuhlp**-tur) an artist who carves or molds shapes

sculpture (**skuhlp**-chur) something carved or molded out of wood, stone, metal, or another material

ANIMALS AT MOUNT RUSHMORE

Mountain Goat

Chipmunk

Turkey Vulture

Porcupine

23

INDEX

FIND OUT MORE

Book:
Bauer, Marion Dane. *Mount Rushmore*. New York: Simon & Schuster, 2007.

Website:
Oh, Ranger!
www.ohranger.com/mount-rushmore

MEET THE AUTHOR
Laine Falk is a writer and Scholastic editor. She lives in Brooklyn, New York, with her family.